Simple Productivity

OrangeBooks Publication

Smriti Nagar, Bhilai, Chhattisgarh - 490020

Website: **www.orangebooks.in**

© Copyright, 2022, Author

All rights reserved. No part of this book may be reproduced, stored in a retrieval system, or transmitted, in any form by any means, electronic, mechanical, magnetic, optical, chemical, manual, photocopying, recording or otherwise, without the prior written consent of its writer.

First Edition, 2022

SIMPLE PRODUCTIVITY

SIMPLE STEPS AND TECHNIQUES YOU CAN IMPLEMENT
TO GET MORE DONE EVEN IF YOU'RE SHORT ON TIME

MUSTAFA MUN

OrangeBooks Publication
www.orangebooks.in

Simple Productivity

Simple Steps and Techniques You Can Implement To Get More Done Even if You're Short on Time

Disclaimer

---

*T*his eBook has been written for information purposes only. Every effort has been made to make this eBook as complete and accurate as possible. However, there may be mistakes in typography or content. Also, this eBook provides information only up to the publishing date. Therefore, this eBook should be used as a guide - not as the ultimate source.

The purpose of this eBook is to educate. The author and the publisher do not warrant that the information contained in this eBook is fully complete and shall not be responsible for any errors or omissions. The author and publisher shall have neither liability nor responsibility to any person or entity with respect to any loss or damage caused or alleged to be caused directly or indirectly by this ebook.

This eBook offers information and is designed for educational purposes only. You should not rely on this information as a substitute, nor does it replace professional medical advice, diagnosis, or treatment.

Table of Contents

Introduction 2

Chapter - 1
Productivity Starts With The Right Mindset 6

Chapter - 2
Create A System And Make It Work For You 11

Chapter - 3
Gather Your Productivity Tools 15

Chapter - 4
Your Day Starts The Night Before 20

Chapter - 5
Your Morning Sets The Tone For The Day 26

Chapter - 6
Eat The Frog! 31

Chapter - 7
Don't Forget To Take Breaks 37

Chapter - 8
Focus And Thrive 43

Conclusion 47

Introduction

Introduction

Welcome to Simple Productivity, an ebook designed to help you maximize your work output while taking care of yourself. In this book, you will find a variety of different time management techniques, morning and night routines, tools, and reminders to help you figure out the productivity system that works best for you!

Whether you have been on the hunt for helpful productivity books for a while or you are brand new to the scene, do not worry. You are going to figure it all out. Besides, this book is here to help guide you along the path of discovering your behaviors, how those behaviors are woven into productivity, and how to create systems that benefit your output as well as your input!

Increasing your productivity can feel like a challenge, especially if you are low on time and motivation. It is a trap that so many of us end up falling into at one point or another during our academic years or our careers. It is easier to push something until later or to find a way to avoid the task altogether, and harder to implement solutions that can increase your productivity.

If this sounds like you, then you are reading the right thing! This ebook is designed to help you find a perfect solution to your lack of productivity. Here, you will discover a variety of different tips, tactics, and tricks to help you utilize your time better and create healthier work and productivity habits!

There are many different kinds of workers, those who are already productive but want more, those who do enough to not be stressed, the procrastinators, the time mismanagers, and others! You might be a mix of several different types of workers, which is why creating a productivity plan for yourself designed to boost your weaknesses into strengths is one of the best things you can do for yourself!

Soon, you will be ready and armed with your own set of routines, techniques, tricks, and tips to maximize your productive output while also increasing your emotional input.

Remember, it is okay to have sluggish days. You are not expected to be productive 24/7. But if you feel that the deadlines are approaching and your to-do list is growing, then you might need some help getting on to the right path. However, you do not need to worry or feel alone. Plenty of people struggle with productivity, and everyone has off days where it seems like nothing gets done. You are not alone! Your friends, coworkers, family, and the barista who makes your coffee have all struggled with feeling unproductive.

Finding the right path can also be tricky, and that is why we are here to guide you. In this ebook, you will learn about many different methods to boost your productivity, keep your sanity, and meet your deadlines! Now, let's not waste any more time with introductions, and let's get straight to the good stuff!

Productivity Starts With The Right Mindset

*A*nything that you want can be changed if you have the right mindset. Your mind is your most powerful tool and your biggest challenger when it comes to productivity. Your mind is the thing that tells you to wait until tomorrow or to watch one more episode instead of starting your work. Your mind is also capable of incredible power to push you in the right direction.

By entering the right mindset, you can set yourself up for success and increase your productivity! Mindset is crucial to beginning to change your work habits and strengthening good work routines as well as kicking unhelpful and unproductive habits and routines to the curb!

But how can you change your mindset? If you are looking for a long-term change, you can change your mindset by creating new neural pathways in your brain related to your workday and productivity by practicing a variety of mindfulness and mental exercises. In the short term, there are a variety of techniques you can use at the moment to help your mindset enter a positive and productive state.

Changing your mindset at the moment is a challenge for some people. However, it is not something to be afraid of! Just as previously stated, your mind is your best tool. You have ownership of your mind. It is yours and, therefore you can create any change you want!

To help create a more positive and productive mindset quickly, try meditation. Meditation may seem like a long-term solution, but taking a moment to reduce your stress through meditation is extraordinarily helpful. Meditation is known to reduce stress, lower blood pressure, help return the body to homeostasis, and even lower the level of the stress hormone cortisol in your body.

This happens all through the breath. Deep and full breathing is a core aspect of meditation and can help oxygenate the blood.

When we get stressed at work, we tense our shoulders, back, or stomach. We begin to take shallower and shorter breaths.

Taking long and slow deep breaths can help increase your blood oxygen levels and increase blood flow to your brain to help sharpen your focus.

Meditation can also be practiced daily to see even stronger long- term results of relaxation and increased focus while working.

Another long-term or short-term practice you can incorporate into your mindset training is yoga! Yoga is not only for flexible people; it is for everyone. A yoga practice can help you increase blood flow around your body which helps increase focus and productivity at work.

It is also great to get your body moving if you feel unproductive! Yoga can help relieve tension in your muscles, which makes you feel better! Yoga is also highly meditative because there is a huge focus on the breath. Yoga is a positive form of movement that can help turn your mindset into a more positive place.

Another way to change your mindset is to change the way you think about work and productivity. If you tell yourself, "I have to do this project and I don't want to," you are going to be unhappy while doing it and avoid starting! You will drag it out because you do not feel like it, and you will make your mindset worse. Try speaking and thinking about your tasks in a more positive way! Try "I get to do this task and show off my skills!"

Changing the way, you think about something will change your mindset over time. You can also change your workspace to be helpful towards your productivity. For example, if you tend to get distracted when you go get a glass of water, then put a glass or pitcher of water in your workspace. Optimizing your workspace for our needs is a way of increasing your positivity in your mindset and helping you get over the productivity block!

Your mindset can and will fluctuate throughout the day, starting clear and typically positive in the morning and tapering into a more negative outlook by early afternoon. Our mindsets can change as easily as the weather, and often change along with our emotions. Mastering how you emotionally relate to your workspace and environment is an integral part of mastering your mindset!

Learn to identify when and why your mood begins to shift throughout the day. Midday burnout? Hungry around 3 but dinner is still hours away? Feeling stiff or cramped at a desk? Identify what brings your mood down and find a solution!

For example, maybe for burnout, keep track of all the things you have done so far! Seeing all you have accomplished that day can give your motivation a boost, which can boost your productivity! If you get hungry (or rather, hangry) after lunch and before dinner, try eating a lunch that is more filling with more protein! Or keep a snack in your workspace. If you get stiff at a desk or workspace, get up! Stretch and walk around for a moment.

Self-awareness and identifying what brings down your productivity is one of the best tools you can have when you begin this journey!

Create a System and Make It Work For You

Create A System And Make It Work For You

People love to share their methods of success with others. They often mean well and tell us their secrets to success as a way of trying to help, but other people's routines and systems are designed for other people, not you! You should create a system that helps you feel good about yourself and your productivity!

Routines are an amazing way to help yourself succeed. It will probably take a bit of time to create a rock-solid routine, but that is okay! Success does not happen overnight, and neither do strong routines.

The best way to start building a routine is piece by piece. Pick one or two things that help you feel good and productive and incorporate them into your work routine. Start with those one or two things and do them every workday. Gradually, you can add new pieces to your routine! Before you know it, you will have created a system of organization and pattern that suits your individual needs!

Of course, it is completely okay to poach habits or organizational tactics from other people, but make sure to tweak and include your organizational routines to make them unique to you.

Creating solid organizational tools that are designed to help strengthen your weaknesses and boost your strengths is a key component to helping your life flow smoothly. For example, if you struggle with time management, create a schedule for yourself that you can use most days. This will not only help you create a stronger routine, but also to help you learn more about time management. You will figure out what takes longer than you thought, what takes less time, and what needs prioritizing.

Organization and routine-making is a lot of trial and error, but eventually, you will find things that help you operate at your best.

Do some research to find organizational techniques or parts of routines that work for you! The first part of finding out what organizational techniques and routines will help you is to become a bit more self-aware.

We all like to think that we are always aware of what we are doing, where we are, and how we are feeling, but that is too much for one person's mind to be juggling all the time. In reality, we are often not as aware as we think we are. Take some time to be aware of yourself. Becoming more self-aware will help you to learn your weaknesses and strengths.

Knowing your weaknesses and strengths is one of the most important parts of creating strong, organized routines and increasing productivity. You should look for things that help strengthen your weaknesses and accentuate your strengths. If you only focus on your weaknesses, you miss out on the opportunity to create stronger skills in your strengths. If you only focus on your strengths, you hold yourself back by not growing as a worker and person.

Learning about your strengths and weaknesses is daunting, but it is not as hard as you think. During a workday or a busy time, take a moment to quickly reflect on how you are feeling, what you are frustrated with, what you are stressed about, and what you are not worried about. Jot it down.

If you do this a couple of times during a workday for several workdays, you should be able to look at what you wrote down and identify patterns of behavior showing you what stresses you, frustrates you, how you feel doing those tasks, and what does not bother you.

So, let's say that you realize you always get stressed about running out of time in your workday as the day begins to end. Maybe you are not managing your time in the morning as best you could, leaving more to do in the latter part of the day, making you feel stressed that you will not get enough done before the workday ends.

Once you recognize your patterns of behavior, you can address them and create systems to help yourself succeed! It will also help to create a seamless flow throughout your day because you will feel more secure, less stressed, and more prepared for each day!

Chapter - 3

Gather Your Productivity Tools

Besides using your mind as a tool of productivity, you can use outside sources to help you become more motivated, organized, and productive. There are so many different tools you can try, make, and incorporate into your workday to make life and productivity easier!

In this digital age, using the tools that our phones, computers, tablets, and smartwatches have is one of the easiest and most helpful things to do! Our electronics are equipped with so much time-saving and productivity-boosting technology right here at your fingertips! Why wouldn't we utilize them?

Computers are a great place to start. Lots of computers have places where you can write notes to yourself, like sticky notes, notepads, or timed messages. You can easily use these note functions to write your lists, jot down something you need to remember, or create a schedule for your day.

If your computer has a reminder function, you can set a timed reminder for certain things. Using these reminders can help you stay on track with your tasks and boost your productivity by helping you remember what needs to be done and stay on task.

Many smartphones also have a reminder function. You can set daily reminders to remind you of daily tasks or special appointment reminders! Some computers and smartphones have built-in reminder options for items that you add to their calendars. Make sure that you choose to opt-in for the reminder. Usually, you can set the reminder to go off a certain amount of time before your engagement or at the moment of.

Calendars, both on and off of devices, are an incredibly useful tool for productivity and maintaining motivation. Calendars show you all the things you have going on in the week or month, which helps you to create priorities, schedule your time, and know what you have coming up on your timeline.

Calendars are also great for tracking habits or behaviors! You can see behavioral patterns by marking the days when you managed your time well or did not feel stressed, or whatever you want to track. At the end of the month, you have a map of your behaviors and habits! You can also track how often you complete and stick to your organizational routines.

You can get a desk calendar, a wall calendar, or a planner with a monthly calendar in it! Planners are a great method of keeping track of day-to-day tasks and to-do lists. Planners usually have a monthly calendar and then each week of that month is broken into 7 daily sections, where you can write down what is planned for each day. Planners like this are great because they help you to see long-term commitments or tasks on the monthly calendar as well as daily and weekly projects.

Planners come in all different styles. You can get planners that have a notes section for each week where you can write down your goals for that week. Some planners have stickers, and other are simple. You can surely find a planner that fits what you are looking for. Make sure that you like your planner because you will be seeing it every day!

Seeing what is ahead of you each month and each week is a really helpful method of long-term time management.

If you are diagnosed with ADHD, (attention deficit hyperactivity disorder) and struggle to remember to take your medication every day, put it in your planner! For people with ADHD, not taking their medication can have intense effects on their productivity, focus, motivation, and job performance. Set yourself up for success by helping yourself remember to take your medication!

If you are more productive when you have coffee, make sure you have a coffee maker on hand! Having a coffee maker around will limit the amount of time you have to go out to buy a cup of coffee. Leaving your workspace to go buy a cup of coffee is not only a time-waster, but it breaks your focus. There are too many motions and processes in buying a cup of coffee to maintain your focus and productive mindset.

So, if coffee helps, keep coffee on hand. If you often get up midday to buy a second cup, bring a thermal bottle to your workspace that has coffee prepared the way you like it inside. A good thermal bottle will keep the coffee hot or cold until you are ready to drink it.

If coffee isn't your vice, locate what makes you break your focus and make sure you keep that thing on hand. That way you get your fix of whatever you need and your productivity, motivation, and focus stay sharp!

Another tool to have on hand other than a coffee pot is a timer. You can get little timers in all shapes and sizes to keep in your workspace. Many phones, smartwatches, computers, and tablets also have timers on them.

This way, you can choose the amount of time that you want to take to complete or start a task, and you know that you will only have the amount you put on the timer to complete it. If you do not complete the task before the timer goes off, take a second to reflect on why. Did you overestimate your ability to finish? Did you get distracted or procrastinate? Why did it take you longer? Find out what happened and try again! Monitor your behaviors and habits so you can change the ones that prevent you from working well.

Your Day Starts the Night Before

Your Day Starts The Night Before

One of the most overlooked but super helpful ways to help increase your productivity and motivation is to set yourself up the night before. In this chapter, we will give you several easy methods and tips to do the night before a workday to have a more productive and effective day!

It is generally known that sleep is an incredibly important part of human life. Sleeping is a key component to increasing productivity, achieving mental clarity, and getting laser-sharp focus. When we sleep, our bodies go into reset mode. All of the information that your brain receives throughout the day is sorted, organized into memories, and stored.

Your brain prunes off neural pathways that you no longer use and strengthens new neural pathways that are being built. Your brain can also make connections between subjects, solve problems encountered during the day, and rest.

Brain activity falls into measurable patterns during deep sleep. At the beginning of sleep, the brain waves slow down and brain activity decreases, allowing your brain to rest from the busy day. Later, in the second and third stages of sleep, the brain experiences quick bouts of brain activity, indicating deep sleep.

In REM sleep and low brain activity sleep is when memories are compounded and stored, cognitive abilities are sharpened and pruned, and you can dream!

Besides your brain, your body also goes through a reset. Digestion, circulation, respiration, and more experience changes that help to keep your body in a healthy state. The cardiovascular system slows down your heart rate and helps regulate your metabolism. Non-REM sleep causes breathing to slow down, and breaths to become deeper and fuller.

Your immune system goes to work clearing out bacteria and viruses, which is why you sleep so often when you are sick. Sleeping allows your body to get rid of harmful cells and things that could hurt your immune system.

Your muscles experience an intense relaxation and your energy level in your body falls drastically, allowing for the body to repair the damage done to the muscles throughout the day. For example, if you worked out that day, you might wake up after a good night's sleep feeling a little sore, which indicates that your muscular system was regenerating cells, creating new cells, and repairing damaged muscle tissue all while you were sleeping!

Hormone levels begin to regulate. The levels of the stress hormone cortisol drop, which is why you can fall asleep worried about something and wake up feeling better about it. Lower cortisol levels can also help your metabolism and immune system function optimally! Melatonin, a hormone related to sleep, increases.

Hormones related to tissue and bone development and growth increase, which helps the muscular system rejuvenate after the day. These same hormones also help the metabolism. The two main hormones that control appetite, ghrelin and leptin, decrease. Good sleep can often help curb cravings and poor eating habits!

These are just some of the amazing benefits of good sleep. Your body is like a machine, without the chance to store data, replace and fix damaged parts, and add system protection, you will fall apart. Your focus and productivity will also decrease, and your stress hormones will increase, which can prevent you from working and sleeping well.

Essentially, the foundation of any strong and productive workday is a strong and productive night's sleep!

Before you run to your bed and try to catch some Z's, you can also physically set yourself up the night before so you can start your morning productively!

If you have a workspace, whether it is in an office or a desk at home, take some time the evening before to clean it up. Get rid of old papers you do not need, wash your coffee mugs and water glasses, put pens away, file papers, and tidy up anything messy.

Making your space clean and ready to go is a perfect way to help yourself be more productive the next day. You won't feel like you have to clean stuff up in the morning, you can just get right to work!

Another way to prep your workspace is to write out your list of things to do the evening before and leave it at your workspace. You can also check your calendar to see if you need to do anything else to prepare for the coming day the night before, so you do not feel pressured or rushed to accomplish it in the morning.

Check your planner and add notes, goals, or words of motivation! Charge your devices completely! That will take a load off in the morning too.

After you have prepped your workspace and before you tuck yourself into bed, create a nighttime routine. This may seem silly or childish, but routines help us more than we know! Night routines are powerful tools in making sure we get everything we want to get done before bed. Night routines also help our bodies and minds to realize that the time for sleep and rejuvenation is coming!

Some things that might be a part of your night routine could be cleaning and prepping your workspace, eating dinner, having tea, stretching or doing a yoga practice, taking a shower or bath, picking out your clothes for the next day, getting in bed to read, and then going to sleep.

Whatever your routine is, make sure you can do it every night! It typically takes about 30 days to create a habit, which is when your brain begins to realize that the pattern means sleep. But you will probably see and experience benefits before 30 days!

Simply having a night routine helps improve sleep and decrease stress. Plus, it is a great way to begin to unwind after your workday! Incorporate things that work for you, start small, and stick to it! You will feel more relaxed at night, sleep better, wake up more refreshed, and have more productivity and focus during the day!

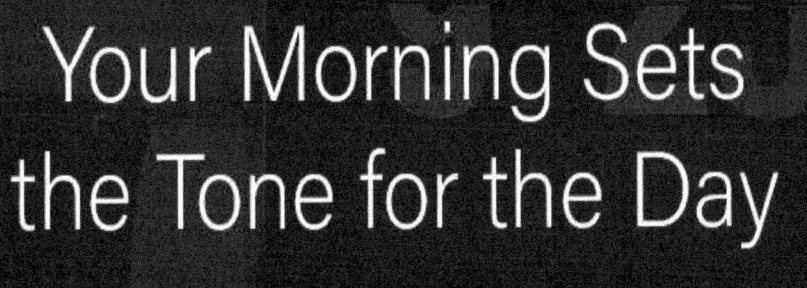

Chapter - 5

Your Morning Sets The Tone For The Day

Just like a night routine, your morning routine is also an important part of setting yourself up for success! No matter what they are for, routines are a great method and tool of switching the brain from one course of action to another. So, a morning routine will help your brain switch from sleep mode to awake and productive mode!

Most of us have morning routines without even realizing it. We wake up, hit snooze, check our phones, emails, and text messages, shower, grab a cup of coffee, and head to work. If that sounds like you, that is great! You have a base to start from.

Most people have short morning routines because they want to maximize the amount of sleep that they are getting. But, if you can have a better night's sleep after implementing a night routine and aiming to get to bed a little bit earlier, you should have no problem waking up a tad earlier to fit in some extra routine aspects to brighten your day and wake up your brain!

Waking up just 15 to 30 minutes earlier in the morning gives your body and mind 15 to 30 minutes to come to life. We have all been there, starting work but our brains feel cloudy, our dreams are still running through our minds, and the coffee is not working. That is your body telling you that it needs more time to get into gear!

Try adding some movement to your mornings. Wake up and move! It seems incredibly difficult, but the movement is one of the easiest and most effective ways to wake your mind and body up! Like we said earlier, you're breathing and heart rate slow down during sleep. They also do not return to normal speed the moment you open your eyes.

Moving your body is the best way to increase circulation, boost your heart rate, get more oxygen into your blood, and feel more awake. Yoga, running, stretching, tai chi, jogging, walking, or light cardio are easy movements that you can include in your morning.

Even if your movement is walking around your house a few times, jogging around the block, doing 10 jumping jacks in your bedroom, or doing a 5-minute yoga sun salutation, your body will feel so much more alive afterward. Touching your toes and reaching above your head is fine too, just get moving!

If you can't add 15 minutes to your morning, try to incorporate movement into the habits and routine you already have. For example, if you make your lunch in the morning, put in headphones or turn on a speaker, play some feel-good music, and dance around the kitchen while you prepare your lunch or breakfast!

Another practice to include in your morning routine is something that makes you feel good. Some people put on a skincare facial mask while they eat breakfast, some people meditate, others say affirmations in front of a mirror. Find a simple self-care act that makes you feel good and make it a part of your morning. You will feel happier and more confident, which will lead to your work ethic, productivity, and motivation getting a great boost!

Good mornings are full of joy, so make a point to find the joyful things. Celebrate something, no matter how small. The sun is out! My cereal is not soggy! I am having a great hair day! My coffee tastes amazing! Whatever brings you joy, identify and take a second to celebrate it.

If you can listen to music in the mornings, make a playlist of feel-good music that gets your energy up! Drink a glass of water before your coffee to help your body wake up from the inside.

Open your curtains and turn on your lights! Bring light into your space to help your energy levels return to normal.

Once you get to your workspace, take a few deep breaths. Help switch your brain to work mode by reading your to-do list, checking your calendar, updating your planner, and opening your email or messages. Doing things like that will help switch your mindset over to work.

It is way harder to jump right into tasks and projects, so give yourself a few moments to breathe and review what the day has in store for you. It will help you feel more in control and also help you prepare or spend your time throughout the day.

One method of reviewing your tasks for the day that can be super fun is the bingo to-do list! Here is how to do it. On a piece of paper, draw a bingo card, (25 squares in one big square, 5x5). In the middle square, write FREE. You get the square just for making this! Then, in the surrounding 24 boxes, randomly write the things from your to-do list. Do not put them in a pattern or a ranked order, just at random.

Add in some fun things you want to do as well. Try to have five nice things. Now, throughout the day, try to get bingo! As you do the items on the bingo card, you get to draw a big X over that task. If you get 5 in a row, you get bingo! If you get bingo, choose a small and simple reward for yourself. Maybe you'll buy yourself a fancy cup of coffee or watch 2 episodes of your favorite show tonight!

Try to find some way of creating fun around your to-do list. You can enjoy challenging yourself and experimenting with other games as to-do lists!

Eat The Frog!

As human beings, we have plenty of things to do each day. Some of those things are far less savory than others. Some are huge and daunting, while others are quick, easy, or fun. But what about those annoying, important, and daunting things? No one wants to do something that does not make them feel happy or good.

That is where the "eat the frog" tactic comes into play! Eat the Frog was inspired by a famous Mark Twain quote, "If it's your job to eat a frog, it's best to do it first thing in the morning. And if it's your job to eat two frogs, it's best to eat the biggest one first." As you have probably guessed, this method has absolutely nothing to do with eating frogs (or any animals,) and all to do with accomplishing the things our psychological and neural emotional centers want to avoid. You can thank the emotional center of our brain for that. Thanks, Amygdala!

Eat the Frog is a tool used by people who struggle with procrastination. Contrary to popular belief, procrastination is not a display of laziness but a psychological avoidance of something unpleasant. A psychologist studying procrastination has found evidence that connects our brains' emotional centers to procrastination.

We avoid doing tasks like writing papers, raking the leaves, doing the laundry, or work-related reports because they do not bring us joy. Our brains fear these tasks because they know that those tasks will not bring a spike of dopamine, the reward and happiness hormone. We avoid tasks to avoid the unpleasant emotions of stress, boredom, or fear of being incompetent.

So how can you beat your brain at its own game? Eat the frog!

The best way to eat a frog? Like Mark Twain said, first thing in the morning! In the morning during your morning routine or once you arrive at your workspace, identify one big task that is both important and something you do not want to do.

Then, do it immediately.

While it seems silly, it is effective! During the day, we are called in all different directions. Our bosses need this, our kids need that, your partner has a question about such-and-such, and your mind is running at a million miles per hour.

In the morning, none of those things had the chance to happen! If the first thing you do is the thing you would avoid all day, you clear up the stress and frustration of dealing with that task once the business of the day picks up.

Eat the frog works because it helps to encourage "deep-work" which is a term used to describe distraction-free work on mentally demanding tasks that use all your attention and skills at once. Eating the frog also works with your agenda, making the item or task you choose a priority. If you choose to eat the frog before engaging with emails or messages from others asking you for your input, you have 100% control of your agenda and attention.

Eating the Frog first thing in the morning is a great way to set you up for success. We often overestimate how much we can get done in a day, which is why we can feel unproductive and then unmotivated by our never-ending to-do lists. By achieving something big and important first, you feel strong and productive! Your mindset becomes more confident and productive as the day continues.

Plus, eating the frog gets those unpleasant tasks out of the way, which reduces stress, fear, and expectation for the rest of the day, which means you will likely feel better throughout the day!

Feeling better and more confident can make you more productive, so give it a shot!

Eat the Frog requires you to focus on one single task, meaning you are focusing on less. While focusing on less may seem unproductive, it has long-term productivity benefits! It means that your work is more precise and focused, and it helps become a powerful motivator as the day continues.

Additionally, the morning hours are often our most productive! Why waste them? In these morning hours, our brains are newly refreshed and our mindset is a positive one. Later in the day our bodies and minds can become worn down, plus our mindset can become more cynical and negative. Take advantage of that positive mindset and fresh brain; just eat the frog!

Lastly, eating the frog is simple. It does not require a billion steps, actions, and choices to work. All it needs is one big, important task that you can get done. It works not only for to-do lists and work assignments; it can work for anything! Let's say you need to clean your room. Start with the thing you do not want to do, maybe laundry or dishes. Once that is done, you can take care of the next frog.

Eating the frog is simple and universal enough to be applied to almost all circumstances or tasks. It is a tactic you can use anywhere, anytime.

Here are some tips for eating your frog. Pick something you can accomplish fully in 1 to 4 hours. Make a goal to finish your frog before lunch so that the rest of the day is clear for other tasks. If your frog is huge, break it into pieces that can be taken in smaller steps. Each step you finish will feel like a win and boost your mindset!

Try not to plan your frog ahead of time. Let your frog show up each morning unexpectedly and then eat it. Do not schedule your frogs out for the week. Just let it occur naturally each morning. You can, however, set yourself up the night before if you need to, just avoid letting your procrastination get in the way.

Procrastination is very common and you are not alone in feeling stuck and unproductive. As long as you want to break out of that pattern and eat some frogs, you will be able to do this!

Remember, it all starts with your mindset!

Don't Forget To Take Breaks

*L*ook, as much as we all want to be superhuman productivity machines, that is not possible. Plus, that would not be a very enjoyable life, now, would it? Breaks are a crucial part of maintaining productivity as well as creating more! Breaks are not weaknesses; they are an important aspect of your workday.

Neuroscience test data shows us interesting information about the human ability to focus and the need for breaks. Humans are cyclical and rhythmic beings, we have internal clocks, our circadian rhythm, our hormonal cycles, digestive cycles, respiratory cycles, and behavioral cycles. Why wouldn't our focus and attention spans have limits and cycles too?

Well, they do! Data shows us that the human mind can maintain undivided attention for approximately 90 minutes. That means you can sit down and do 90 minutes of work with minimal internal distractions. After those 90 minutes, your attention begins to fade and become brittle.

Fragile attention spans are more likely to be broken by simple things, like a phone ringing or a coworker asking a question. We can get irritated, worn out, and stressed-out way easier when we are pushing ourselves past our natural attention spans.

It is a good thing, though, that we are creatures of cycles! After a short 20-to-30-minute break, our attention is ready to go again! However, your break has to be unrelated to attention. You can't shift over to another task to take a break from another. That defeats the purpose.

Take your eyes away from whatever you are doing, change the view, play a silly game, have a snack, get some water, make some tea, go for a quick walk. Let your system reboot the attention cycle and you will find yourself feeling way more refreshed when you come back the task at hand.

One great method for remembering to take breaks and taking those breaks effectively is the Pomodoro method! The Pomodoro method is a super easy and effective time management system that helps you to see how much time you spending on tasks, as well as take timed breaks to recharge your mental attention!

The Pomodoro method breaks down your day into 25-minute sections with planned and timed breaks. Here is how it works. When you sit down to begin a task or project or your workday, set a timer for 25 minutes. When the timer goes off, you get to have a five-minute break! Once the five minutes are up, you set the timer for another 25 minutes!

At the end of each 25-minute Pomodoro, you get a five-minute break. After 4 cycles, (four 25-minute Pomodoro work periods and 4 five-minute breaks), you get to take a 20 to 30-minute break!

With this method, you get approximately 100 minutes of work in, 20 minutes of spaced-out breaks, and then a nice chunk of time for recharging and relaxing.

The Pomodoro technique is very helpful for people who struggle with time management. Not only because the Pomodoro technique helps to section out your day, but also because after the timer goes off for each 25-minute work period, you can see how much work you got done in that time. Maybe you can notice patterns about your work like maybe this task is taking longer than you expected!

The Pomodoro technique is great for fidgety kids, energetic adults, people with ADHD, and those who have poor time management.

There are also several signs that you can look for that may indicate it is time for a break. These signs are as follows: fidgeting, nervous energy, getting distracted by outside forces easily, zoning out or daydreaming, getting frustrated when something does not work out immediately, making silly mistakes, feeling eye fatigue, and other physical indications that you are wearing yourself out.

When you realize it is time for a break, take one! Whether you are using the Pomodoro technique or not, get up out of your chair, stretch, walk around, get some water or coffee, use the restroom, and say hi to a coworker!

Make your break from working something simple and easy that you can do quickly that can also reset you! Your breaks should not be stressful or intense, so do not try to cram something into a five-minute break if it does not fit.

For example, do not try to cook and eat lunch in-between Pomodoros! Five minutes is simply not enough time, no matter how quickly you think you can go. You will most likely stress yourself out and still be hungry. Grab a snack instead, or start part of the cooking process! When the next pomodoro ends, you can continue!

Having appropriate breaks that switch your mind off of work will help you to feel way more refreshed when the next Pomodoro begins!

Another way to incorporate breaks into your workday is to have a set time each day when you step back and take a break.

Maybe you tell yourself that after 3 hours at your workspace, you will take a moment to stretch and get water. Maybe you tell yourself that after you accomplish something on your task list, you will go for a quick walk or have a snack if you are hungry.

Some people will take a longer break after every 5 items they cross off their to-do list. Others will have a buddy who takes a break at the same time they do, so they can both relax and reset together!

The buddy method is a great way to remember to take breaks while having some social time. It also helps your brain switch from work mode to something relaxing and enjoyable. When the break ends, you will find your mind feeling a bit crisper than it was when you started the break. Even if you and your buddy just sit in silence and have a snack.

Focus and Thrive!

Focus And Thrive

There are some important things to remember when you begin to try and increase your productivity. First, you are trying.

Remember that you are trying something new! These habits and techniques are new to you, and even if you have heard of them before, they are still new in your life at this moment.

You are trying. The first step is trying to decide that you want to! You have made that first step by reading this. You are spending your time wisely to try to become a better version of yourself tomorrow, and that is incredible!

Trying inevitably means falling short sometimes. You are not perfect, but you are beginning a new journey of self-discovery and progress. Progress is the best you can do, whether it is big or small. Progress is progress, and you should be proud of yourself for each step you take towards it!

Secondly, you are on a journey to discover what works for you. Not everything that works for other people will automatically work for you. You may have to change some things, get rid of others, and add your flair to other techniques. Do not be afraid to adapt both productivity systems and yourself to make things work.

Life is about being flexible and focused, so regardless of whether you alter some of these techniques to work for you, your focus must not falter or change. Stay focused on your goals, live into them with all you've got!

Focus is also heavily reliant on the systems you decide to utilize. You might load your plate up too high at the start and realize that you can't handle it. That is okay! Adjust your plans or goals to work for you.

Do not beat yourself up for needing to adjust your plans. That is okay! You are experimenting to find out what works! Plus, what works for 4 months might need to be changed when your projects change, or your workplace changes! Life is full of unexpected changes, so do not panic when change inevitably comes.

Maybe instead of resisting change, we can welcome it as a new adventure, something to be excited about! Something that will help us adapt to new parts of our lives.

Do not fear or defend against change, let it come in. The change will help you create the perfect productivity system for you! You are your best guide, teacher, and motivator. If mastering your mindset, motivation, and productivity sounds like something only Nobel Prize winners can do, well anyone can!

Just keep your focus on why you are doing this.

You are doing it for you! Focus on how you will feel when one day you realize that your sleep, your mornings, and your workdays are a more pleasant and productive experience. You can and will continue to thrive by focusing on the good.

Lastly, remember that productivity is not everything. You are not a robot, you are not perfect, and you do not have to be productive every second of every day. It is okay to have rough days where you do not get all the things on your to-do list done. That is normal and natural!

Life is unpredictable, so you will not always have the ability to do everything according to plan. Allow the unexpected, take a deep breath, and remind yourself that you are human. If you begin to get incredibly stressed out over productivity, that is a sign you should take a break from planning your productivity and plan out your next chance to relax.

Make sure you allow yourself to thrive during this journey. Nothing is worth hurting yourself over. Becoming the most productive version of yourself is also becoming the healthiest and most self-aware version of yourself. Self-awareness means knowing when to take a break and try again later. It means quitting sometimes, not always, and only when it is hurting you not to.

You have saddled up your horse of success. Now ride off into the sunset!

Conclusion

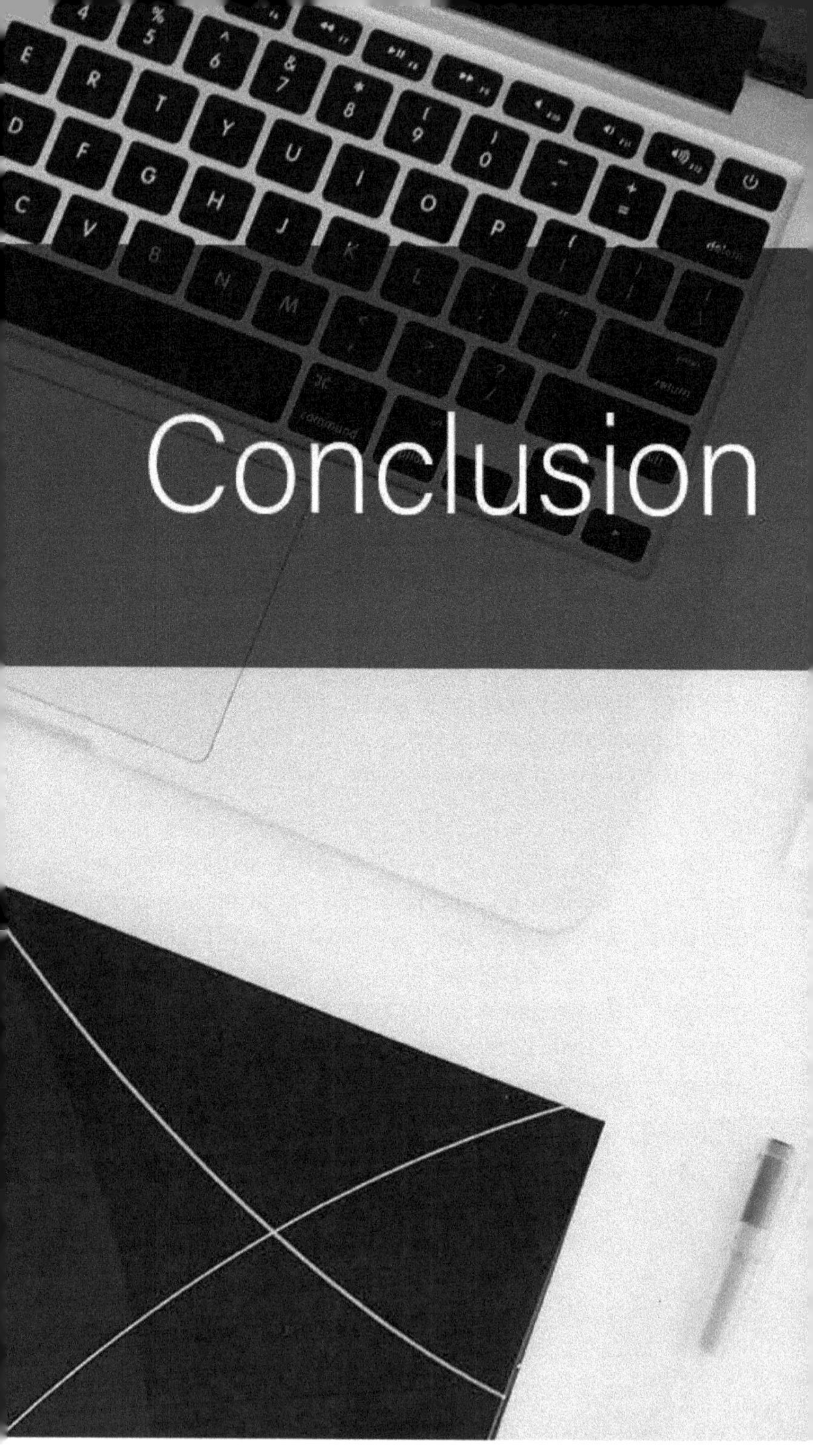

Conclusion

*W*ell reader, here we are. We have reached the end of simple productivity. You have been given the necessary skills and techniques to create healthy, happy, and productive working patterns.

The next steps are in your hands. You have chosen to better your productivity and life once already, and that led you here. The next level is up to you! You are the one in control now, so stay focused on achieving your dreams and goals! Stick to these techniques and find new ones that also work for you. Do what you need to do to make your life better and easier.

Be proud of this! You took the time to read this and you made the decision to better your work and productivity throughthe application of new techniques, and you made the decision to learn new things. You are the one who is implementing new routines, healthier habits, and using knowledge of yourself to create the life that you want.

You deserve a pat on the back! Even though you are just getting started, you have already accomplished so much! Now, you can begin to make a to-do list of night routines, morning routines, and productivity tools! Set your timer for a pomodoro and let's go.

Just don't forget to take a deep breath first!

www.ingramcontent.com/pod-product-compliance
Lightning Source LLC
LaVergne TN
LVHW061603070526
838199LV00077B/7160